Frank Lloyd Wright
AT A GLANCE

INTERIORS

Frank Lloyd Wright
AT A GLANCE

INTERIORS

Abby Moor

PRC

This edition first published in 2001 by
PRC Publishing Ltd,
8–10 Blenheim Court, Brewery Road, London N7 9NY
A member of the Chrysalis Group plc

Distributed in the U.S. and Canada by:
Sterling Publishing Co., Inc.
387 Park Avenue South
New York, NY 10016

ISBN 1 85648 595 1

Printed and bound in China

Page iii: The Lowell E. Walter House, also known as "Cedar Rock," in Cedar
Rock, Iowa, exemplifies the Usonian Home, conceived by Wright after the
Great Depression. These simple, yet beautifully designed houses were
inexpensive structures which responded to modern lifestyles. See page 48.

ACKNOWLEDGMENTS

The publisher wishes to thank Simon Clay for taking all the photography in
this book, including the cover photography, with the following exceptions:

© Richard Bryant/Arcaid for pages 33, 34 and 35 (both);
© Bettmann/Corbis for back cover (top).

CONTENTS

1

INTRODUCTION

Frank Lloyd Wright has often been called an architect of genius. His architectural vision was both bold and pioneering and much of what he did in a building, whether of the domestic, public, or religious type, was ahead of its time. His early work looked forward to most of the dominant concerns of the Modern Movement, while consistently pushing the boundaries of late-nineteenth and early-twentieth century architectural conservatism in America. His later work determined many of the key architectural themes to emerge in the post-World War II era both in Europe and the United States.

Among all the things which can be said about Wright, one of the most important is that he retained the integrity of his own architectural philosophy throughout his long career. From early on in his work, a number of key commitments were apparent. Although maturing and evolving over the course of the years, these themes remained the foundation stones, as it were, of Wright's achievement and were never compromised. They include his fundamental respect for nature as the source of all architectural form, his Arts & Crafts belief in the "honest" expression of materials, and his interest in the progressive use of technology in architecture. At the forefront of his philosophy there was also a daring and innovative treatment of open-plan living spaces in domestic buildings. Certainly in America, this new type of living space changed the very nature of residential interior design forever.

Wright built hundreds of houses for private clients. In each instance he conscientiously readdressed the fundamental principles of his philosophy of "organic" architecture. This meant the unique distribution of interior spaces in relation to each site and each ground plan. It meant an unusual attention to all interior detailing, the sensitive selection of materials, an integrated treatment of ornamentation, and an adventurous variation in the interior elevations within a single dwelling. Above all, it meant for Wright that the interior of a home was more than a metaphorical "shelter." It was the very core space for the realization of family life, and at its center he consistently situated the hearth.

RIGHT: Unitarian Meeting House interior elevation with balconies rising above podium.

ABOVE: Karen Johnson House hallway with flooring/windows/cabinets.

Although enrolled for a short period at undergraduate level in engineering school, Wright began his professional architectural career as chief draughtsman in the Chicago architectural firm of Adler & Sullivan in 1889. Through his own lectures and publications, the Chicago-based architect Louis Sullivan (1856–1924) was already becoming the most ardent spokesman and theorist of the new "organic" architecture. The influence of this concept on the young Frank Lloyd Wright was crucial, and located his most formative aesthetic influences within the movement for reform within all of the applied and design arts.

The design reform movement of the 1880s and 1890s, in both Britain and the United States, called for a new "vernacular" architecture. It advocated the revival of local and regional building traditions because these represented the most "honest" expression of local needs, materials, and the historic past. This reforming doctrine came to be called "fidelity to place." It condemned the tradition of architectural symmetry and proportion, offering instead a new emphasis on the use of indigenous materials, a unique responsiveness to each individual site, and attentiveness to individual clients' needs.

In the American middle western states this emerging style of building came to be known as the "Prairie School" and its most historically important advocate has now become Frank Lloyd Wright. But Wright was not merely another practitioner of another new architectural style. He shared his vision with a loosely-knit group of architects who all sought an original, typically regional approach to building. They desired a style which would be at once ahistorical and an ideal expression of the American middle west. The spirit and expanse of the prairie landscape thus became metaphors of their new architectural identity.

Wright had also been deeply influenced by earlier ninteenth-century architectural theorists, such as John Ruskin, Viollet-le-Duc, and Owen Jones. But perhaps more adamantly than these forebears Wright advocated design based entirely upon the structures and "spirit" of nature. For him, all the supposedly disparate factors of a building, including its siting, elevation, ground-plan, structure, materials, ornamentation, and even its most minute detail, should be interrelated, reflecting the unifying "organic" principles of nature. As a result of this philosophy of "organic" architecture, from the exterior Wright's buildings appear to emerge effortlessly from their site. Their materials correspond to local surroundings, and their

ABOVE: Robert G. Walton House dining room.

forms harmonize with the characteristics of the regional landscape. Wright's questioning of the very character of residential architecture led to equally innovative interior spaces. Naturalness and simplicity for him meant the elimination of anything nonessential within the home. He was also determined to eradicate what he considered the artificial "box-like" division of rooms in conventional Victorian interiors.

While at Adler & Sullivan, Wright contributed to the firm's design of domestic residences, already beginning to establish a body of work which would generate the greatest portion of his future livelihood. His relationship with Sullivan ended in 1893, however, as a result of disputes over the so-called "bootlegged" houses which Wright had designed in his own time, but while employed by the firm. Sullivan's influence nevertheless is readily apparent in details of residences such as the Blossom House of 1892.

ABOVE: Eric V. Brown House sitting room.

After leaving Adler & Sullivan, Wright continued to work primarily in the realm of domestic architecture and in the suburbs of Chicago, notably in Oak Park. There he continued to add to his own residence, which became his office and studio as well as his home, and he developed the fully-fledged Prairie House style for which he is now so well known. Beginning with his Oak Park residence, commenced in 1889, Wright dramatically reduced the public formality of the ground floor rooms. He also decreased their number to only those absolutely necessary. Thereafter, his houses would consistently contain spacious living and dining rooms, as well as kitchens (with ancillary utility rooms) as the elementary modules of any ground floor interior.

His preference for simplicity led him to build these rooms around the central core of the fireplace. Wright saw the domestic residence as a sanctuary. Extensive use of masonry, concentrated in the hearth (which anchored the building to the earth), represented an almost elemental sense of security and protection. It focused the experience of the home inward, toward family life, while the static, monolithic formality of much of Wright's furniture design, most notably for the dining room, signified the sanctity of family ceremony. In the Prairie-style houses, such as the Francis W. Little "1" House of 1902 and the Darwin Martin complex of 1903–04, his earliest arrangement of rooms was often cruciform, with the hearth centralized in the plan. But in the later I-plan Usonian houses the hearth became the focal point of a more longitudinal arrangement, with rooms moving in a line away from it or, as in the L-shaped Usonians, placed at the axis where the two wings joined.

Most of the Prairie-style houses, were built during the period 1899 to 1910. In their elongated masses of low-lying masonry, their forceful overhanging eaves, and the rigorous horizontal windows, residences such as the Susan Lawrence Dana House of 1902 appear to unfold from the ground beneath. Inside, Wright also began to omit the conventional walls between rooms—an essential part of the destruction of the "box," which is a highly visible departure from convention within the Dana House interior. By abolishing walls, Wright opened-up rooms which could then project into one another, as well as overlap. Boundaries became established by daily use and habit. Wright also liked to design built-in cupboards, sideboards, and low-hung, screen-like partitions which cleverly alluded to the conventional separations between spaces, for example within a stairwell, but failed to interrupt the pleasure of unrestricted views.

Wright's development of interiors was greatly governed by his personal response to natural materials. These always remained in as natural and unshrouded a state as possible. His woods were never concealed beneath varnish; merely stained. Concrete was left exposed and unadorned. The prominence of masonry—that is, stone and brick—in his designs could not be undervalued, for these materials regularly carried the strongest impact of texture and color in his interiors.

Unusually for architects of his time, Wright was also remarkably oriented toward drawings-based planning, facilitating the ease with which he was able to turn to manufacturers to fit out his interiors. Not adverse to the use of the machine, Wright on the contrary applauded it as "of our time" and made use of its ability to democratize and "industrialize" the execution of residential interiors.

Wright's experimentation with technological innovation is well known through his use of the so-called concrete "textile blocks" in the California residences of 1923 and after. The concrete blocks from which, for example, the John Storer House was fabricated were not only comparatively inexpensive, but cast in individual moulds on site. They were then joined together with steel rods and concrete grout which acted as a mortar course. Even within the scheme for an individual building, these blocks were cast in differing surface patterns: some carried glass insets, while others were either perforated or cast as solid modules. The resulting sculptural potential for an ornamentally co-ordinated interior space was pioneering. The perforated blocks forced the movement of daylight and shadow into a complex variety of patterns filtering through to the interior. This in part diminished the absolute necessity of windows for light and ventilation. Windows themselves, then, became an increasingly strategic part of any aesthetic statement in a design as Wright further experimented with the interplay between interior and exterior views. The interior wall surfaces of these houses became masterpieces of patterned sculptural relief which had no precedent in the history of American domestic architecture.

Wright also typically designed the furniture, fixtures, and fitting for all his houses, eventually also contributing tableware and textiles. Many of his residences became as well-known for their sophisticated design-informed furnishings as for their distinctive architecture. Especially in the later Usonian houses, dating from the 1930s onward, his furnishings were adapted to the straight-line, clean-cutting abilities of machine production, but were unheralded in their functionality and simplicity of form. In fact, Wright's advocacy of machine-cut wood and, eventually, of pre-cut components that could be assembled by clients themselves to his design specifications, was no less than a watershed in the execution of bespoke house design.

Wright's residences also contained significant symbolic content from the outset. His symbolism was in some respects the most potent factor in his interiors. The pervading earth tones found from the Prairie houses through to the late, seminal projects such as Taliesin West not only signified the earth, but were co-ordinated to harmonize with each and every regional location.

While buildings dating up to about 1910 established the theoretical and, in many respects, the practical boundaries within which his interior design would continue to evolve, his later work was by no means a simple restatement of those achievements. In structures designed for the purposes of worship Wright virtually changed the course of religious architecture in America. Beginning with the Unity Temple of 1905, and continuing through to his later projects such as the Pilgrim Congregational Church of 1958, sensitivity to the site and to the client were of paramount importance. With its site situated within the urban sprawl, the Unity Temple, for example, is cocooned within innovative, non-supportive wall "screens" of poured concrete, which Wright stretched upward to the cantilevered roof. The temple is thus conscientiously buffered against urban sound, and the interior lit by a series of coffered skylights with a narrow band of windows hidden just beneath the eaves. The interior thus takes on a solemn and transcendental quality typical of Wright's vision.

In the end, interiors designed by Frank Lloyd Wright retained their conservative, protective function despite their innovations. His natural and lifelong affinity to geometric shape was visible in both space and form, while his early affiliation with the reforming Arts & Crafts movement in America was amply demonstrated by his struggle for greater simplification and integration within every interior. He allowed nothing unsympathetic; nothing which might cause interference with the totality of the broad composition. Each interior design by Wright was a further vindication of his belief that an indigenous, uniquely American form of architectural expression was possible.

2

CASE STUDIES

FRANK LLOYD WRIGHT
HOME AND STUDIO

Constructed: 1889–1909

Address: 951 Chicago Avenue, Oak Park, Illinois 708-848-1976.

Opening hours: Tours Monday to Friday 11am, 1 & 3pm; Saturday and Sunday 11am–4pm.

In 1889 Wright signed a contract with the Chicago architectural firm of Adler & Sullivan, beginning a six-year tenure with the firm, initially as a draughtsman. In the same year he borrowed $5,000 from Sullivan, enabling him to purchase land and construct a home for his wife and future children. That property became his Oak Park residence until 1909, having been added to and remodeled over the course of twenty years. It is a monument to the evolution of Wright's concept of personal, interior space, and effectively became a "laboratory" for his ceaseless experimentation.

The first plan saw the central living spaces spiral outward from the inglenook fireplace which Wright had placed centrally in the plan as the focal point of domestic life. The symbolic theme of the masonry core was perhaps the single most important *leitmotif* in Wright's architectural career. Over the next seventy years he would alter interior arrangements considerably, but the notion that the family gathered about the symbolic, sacred hearth was a mainstay. In the early years, as at Oak Park and throughout the Prairie House period, the hearth typically took the form of an inglenook and occupied a slightly set back, private niche of its own. In the Oak Park house it appears prominently for a second time on the same property in the barrel-vaulted children's playroom which Wright added in 1895.

RIGHT: The west end of the playroom, which became a gathering place for children from throughout the neighbourhood. During the remodelling campaign, Wright created this new space within the second story of the house, yet its own interior is nearly two-stories high. From the built-in window benches, which also doubled as storage space for toys, the children looked directly into the boughs of the trees, giving the large room the feel of a secret playhouse in the woods. The mural atop the arched brick fireplace depicts the legend of "The Fisherman and the Genie" from the *Arabian Nights*.

A profoundly felt sentiment for the family as the *raison d'être* of domestic architecture influenced many aspects of the Oak Park interior. In the dining room there is a new harmony and spaciousness, which contradict the cramped formality of Victorian tradition. Yet the hovering, protective quality of the ceiling and the tall, enclosing chairs give the room something of a liturgical character. Following the introduction of the high-backed, slatted dining chair at Oak Park, the design quickly became another distinctive mark of Wright's style. Its method of slatted, vertical construction closely resembles Wright's use of the slatted screen or partition in later houses. It becomes clear he intended the sheltering arrangement of chairs around the table to create a sense of intimacy and enclosure for the family gathering. Throughout the house there is already an indication of Wright's growing desire for the liberation of box-like spaces and for the sympathetic use of natural materials. Broad openings between the living and dining rooms, and the entry and hallways, allow the rooms to flow into one another. Surfaces show their natural grains and textures, and wood already predominates.

ABOVE RIGHT: The living room demonstrates Wright's architectural intentions toward the opening up and simplification of domestic space. There are plain geometric shapes to the windows. Anything that might hide the structural clarity of the room, such as wallpaper, is cast aside. The whole composition of the interior has become measured and becalmed.

RIGHT: In the dining room, the combination of both artificial and natural light sources were to be another key theme of Wright's career. Oak Park was the first instance in which he so boldly experimented with combining these two sources through the use of a deep clerestory bay combined with the signature recessed lighting grille which radiated indirect, or as he called it, "moonlight."

LEFT: The quiet simplicity of the ground floor interior is also apparent in the bedrooms above where, again, the ceiling is given a distinct structural and ornamental personality much informed by the Arts and Craft movement.

SUSAN LAWRENCE DANA HOUSE (DANA-THOMAS HOUSE)

Constructed: 1902–04

Address: Dana–Thomas House State Historic Site, 301 East Lawrence Avenue, Springfield, Illinois, 62703.

Opening hours: Guided tours 9am–4pm Wednesday to Sunday, about every 20 minutes.

Telephone: 217-782-6776

This was the first commission received by Wright in which finances as such were not an issue. The Prairie-style house Wright designed for the fashionable and socially prominent Susan Lawrence Dana resulted in a building comprising 12,000 square feet and 35 separate rooms distributed over three primary levels and sixteen subsidiary ones. The building's imposing horizontal mass demonstrated both the status and design-awareness of its owner. The extant collections of Wright-designed art-glass and furniture contained here prove the extent to which this extravagant commission allowed Wright, for the first time, to design a thoroughly integrated Prairie School ensemble uniting the decorative arts within an original architectural setting. In fact, with its concentration on interior space, the Lawrence Dana house is in many respects the quintessential Prairie School residence. Ceiling heights vary in order to suggest the functional differences between otherwise interpenetrating spaces. Individual "rooms" are given their personality by unified "organic" surface treatment, such as wood paneling. Unexpected vistas are created throughout by the careful manipulation of light and shadow. As later in the Aline Barnsdall "Hollyhock" House, here Wright used ornamental motifs inspired by

RIGHT: The sumptuous interiors of the Lawrence Dana House demonstrate Wright's total intergration of architecture, furnishings, and decorative arts. In excess of 450 pieces of art glass and over 100 pieces of oak furniture were designed and produced by the architect and his studio over two years.

nature to unify the interior composition. These motifs are evident in the running frieze of the dining room balcony where the indigenous sumac combines with the purple aster to give the house its decorative theme. The same motifs, joined by the golden rod, appear elsewhere in the house and often, most notably in the many abstract motifs in the art-glass. The interior also holds many spatial surprises. Niches appear unexpectedly as one "room" space blends into another. Balconies, like that running beneath the barrel vault of the dining room, give an unusual perspective from which to view Wright's spaces. The overall design of the interior was clearly meant by Wright to not only be seen, but experienced first-hand by walking through the different spaces of the house.

LEFT: This photograph of the hearth at the Lawrence Dana House also gives an indication of Wrightian spaces flowing effortlessly into each other.

ABOVE RIGHT: One example of the collaboration with the sculptor Richard Bock in the completion of the interior is the unusual fountain "Moon Children" integrated into the wall of the building. Bock also contributed other pieces to the decorative scheme, although the fountain is perhaps the most important because, along with the plants it serves, it symbolically redressed the absence of significant foliage on this urban site.

RIGHT: The art glass in the Lawrence Dana House, featuring the recurring motifs of butterflies and sumac, is magnificent.

LAWRENCE MEMORIAL LIBRARY

Constructed: 1905
Address: Lawrence Mata Simpson Resource Center, 101 East Laurel, Springfield,
Illinois, 62704.
Opening hours: Open during library hours: 9am–7pm, Monday–Friday.
Telephone: 217-525-3144

The interior of the Lawrence Memorial Library, its furnishings, fixtures and fittings were also commissioned by Susan Lawrence Dana, and intended as a tribute to her late father, a former president of the Springfield School Board. Originally constructed in the Lawrence School, south of the Dana Lawrence House, the library was dismantled and stored during the 1930s, and finally restored in 1992. Its plan and many details closely resemble those of Susan Lawrence Dana's own private library in her nearby home, including the oak spindle-backed chairs. Here, the more substantial bookcases are placed at an angle coming forward from the window wall where there are alcoves between the shelving for public seating. An oak-spindled balustrade divides the length of the space between the bookcases and the reading room, seperating the different functions fulfilled by the different spaces of the single large room.

RIGHT: The reading room of the Lawrence Memorial Library with the Wright-designed library tables and chairs.

EDWIN H. CHENEY HOUSE

Constructed: 1903
Address: 520 North East Avenue, Oak Park, Illinois.
Opening hours: The house is currently run as a Bed and Breakfast for which
reservations are required.
Telephone: 708-524-2067

This is a slightly compressed version of the single-story, square-planned Prairie House. It is an excellent example of Wright's modification of his designs to suit the middle-priced market and to experiment with combining the Prairie House aesthetic with a more condensed bungalow-type structure. Because this brick house has a basement, atypical of the normal Prairie plan, the entryway at the side is raised upon a narrow stylobate which increases the structure's marked sense of seclusion, both inside and out. The interior is something of an alternative scheme, but remains highly economical in its spatial arrangements. The front is given over to a living room which extends from side-to-side the length of the building. Its windows are raised above normal level, blocking the view of passers-by and, as in the Unity Temple of 1905, lessening any intrusion of noise from outside. An ample stone hearth is centralized in the plan, but behind it Wright placed a long gallery which also runs the length of the house and effectively divides the interior into two separate halves. Bedrooms are situated at the rear. Ornamentation as such is negligible, but, a number of important features define the character of the spaces. Wright stipulated the wood trim was not to be waxed, but unusually given a reddish

RIGHT: Even in the earlier houses Wright had begun to perforate the upper elevations of interior walls with viewing niches, creating vistas through the depth of the house and prefiguring his later dissolution of the "box" altogether.

stain. The ceiling rests upon a wooden base. From this base, darkened beams project gently upward to form the underside of a long, tent-like gable. The masonry hearth is an inglenook, typical of this period of Wright's career. Its heavy mass functions as a wall in its own right, while the living spaces open up away from it, toward both sides of the house. The changing angles of the ceiling beams give both pattern and texture to the upper spaces of the room, and help to lower the apparent ceiling height. The result is that the room seems to be compressed outward. Many of the original built-in furnishings and storage units remain intact. Even today they help to open up the interior by forcing weight and volume to the sides of each room. The design of the interior is focused on strong horizontals. Wright was engaged on this residence when he met Mamah Borthwick Cheney with whom he subsequently had a lengthy affair which only ended in her tragic death at Taliesin East in 1914.

ABOVE RIGHT: The bedrooms of Wright's houses tended to be simplified and comfortable, with the banding of wooden trim providing the only decorative features but for the art-glass.

RIGHT: The dining room is also located in the front of the house, opening up off of the living room. Its in-built sideboard is compact and functional, and is constructed as an integral part of the building. Windows are raised well above ground level, insulating the rooms from disturbances outside.

ABOVE: The living areas extend the length of the building along the whole of the front.

ALINE BARNSDALL HOUSE ("HOLLYHOCK HOUSE")

Constructed: 1917
Address: 4808 Hollywood Boulevard, Los Angeles, California.
Opening hours: The house and property are undergoing restoration
and will not reopen until 2004.
Telephone: 213-485-4581

Unquestionably, one of Wright's most famous residences, the so-called "Hollyhock House" was designed for the California heiress and theater producer Aline Barnsdall. Meeting Wright in 1914, the client imagined building what amounted to a small urban center on her own Los Angeles property, incorporating residential and retail spaces. Eventually the majority of the project was dropped, but Wright did execute two small guest houses in addition to the extraordinary large house which was constructed of poured concrete blocks in both low and high relief. The ornamental theme of the hollyhock was the patron's favorite flower, but the treatment of the theme was purely Wright. His work was inspired by pre-Columbian, specifically Mayan, antiquities which he had studied earlier. The theme permeates every surface of the house, and led to perhaps one of the most complete, albeit extravagant, realizations of integrated "organic" ornament achieved in Wright's career.

In plan, the Barnsdall house is reminiscent of the Italian architecture Wright experienced first-hand while traveling in Italy half a decade earlier. Characteristically the house revolves outward from the substantial living room and hearth. The adjacent library and music room spaces grow out of this, while additional rooms

RIGHT: The "hollyhock" motif sets the theme of the residence, and is visible even in the smallest details of the rich interior, including in the patterning of the carpet designed by Wright. Not least in Wright's design of the furnishings, the house has a marked early modern ethos. This is also seen in the value he placed on acknowledging the spatial "void," and in offsetting the symmetry of the intricate hollyhock pattern with broad open areas of plain surface and empty space.

are located in the wings which reach out laterally in both directions. Directly in front of the hearth there is an indoor reflecting pool which mimics the circular pool in the garden courtyard outside. There is also evidence here of how easily Wright could reshape his own established architectural themes. In front of the hearth there is a variation on the built-in settle of his Prairie houses. The sofa (reproduced here from the original) with its solid wooden-slatted back echos the inglenook fireplace of the Prairie-house interior. The sofa—which becomes a table and lamp at one end—wraps itself around the hearth, forming a protective niche. Its shape is the abstract "hollyhock" of the house, but here receives three-dimensional, spatial expression. In the furnishings and wall treatments the screen motif which Wright had often used before is also repeated.

ABOVE RIGHT: The dining room furniture is monolithic in its harsh verticality. This is especially evident in the chair backs. With their integrated relief decoration these recall carved stone artefacts of pre-Columbian origin.

RIGHT: Perhaps unusually for Wright, the living area leads onto a walled courtyard of distinctly Italian inspiration.

LEFT: The massive overmantle of the stone fireplace has a low decorative relief representing the hollyhock, Aline Barnsdall's favorite flower. The face of the stone also steps back in a series of low planes, balancing the busy decorative patterning with plain surfaces. There is a shallow reflective pool at the base, repeating on the interior one of the major themes of the exterior garden and integrating the two "living" spaces as one.

JOHN STORER HOUSE

Constructed: 1923
Address: 8161 Hollywood Boulevard, Los Angeles, California.

One of Wright's four "textile-block" houses executed in California. Along with the Millard, Ennis, and Freeman houses, this building was remarkably forward thinking for its era in the United States. It represented Wright's ongoing ambition to create an innovative and, in some respects, unprecedented domestic architectural style which he could claim as genuinely American in character. For use as the dominant materials Wright developed perforated modules of precast concrete blocks with embossed patterns on more than one face. This insured an equally rich textural interest to the wall surfaces both inside and out. It also incorporated Wright's philosophy of the 'new age' of the machine into his development of unique building materials. These concrete blocks, which were assembled using steel rods and reinforcing poured concrete, represented an entirely new approach to architecture. It is not surprising that a construction technique such as this, born of Wright's continual experimentation, was pioneering it its effect on the quality and distribution of natural light in the interior. In plan, the house had two stories. In one wing there were bedrooms, but these were distributed over two levels. Utilities, including the kitchen, were in the other wing. Both wings extend outward from the center

RIGHT: The Storer house was the second of Wright's textile-block houses. The interior wall surfaces were his most highly textured to date and had been prefigured by his innovations at Hollyhock.

of the building containing the living areas. The dining area is on the ground floor, while the living room is raised above to take advantage of the view over the city. The two floors are connected by a winding stair that forces the onlooker to experience a variety of vistas while climbing through different levels of the building. In the living room, the hearth is a massive structure of alternating textures with a slightly protruding overmantel. The room space is equally tall and wide. It extends out onto a terrace and is also lit by windows along two opposite sides. Its dominant verticality is checked by the ceiling beams, which lead the eye back downward into the cool depths of the room. The original furnishings, which remain in the house, are genuinely exquisite, with a predominant geometric shape as well as a great delicacy of ornamentation and rich contrast of materials and color.

ABOVE RIGHT: Light filtering through the blocks creates a geometric patterning in the interior and a truly "integral" ornamentation in the building. The blocks also afford plenty of light, but at the same time protect the interior from the harsher direct light of the midday sun.

RIGHT: The interior is comprised of rows of textile-block piers, often paired, with concrete benches buttressing the interior space below and curtains of clear glazed panels resting in between.

ABOVE: A view into the dining area illustrates the cool, temple-like environment of the house. Broad vistas of open space help to keep the house cool by affording ample circulation, indirect light, and pockets of shade.

STANLEY ROSENBAUM HOUSE

Constructed: 1939.

Address: 601 Riverview Drive, Florence, Alabama

Initially designed as an L-shaped Usonian house, further additions were implemented by Wright himself in 1948, resulting in a U-shaped building enclosing a sizeable garden. It was the first of the Usonian houses to be substantially altered in this way. The house was subsequently renovated in 1970, but continues to be considered a very pure example of the Usonian type.

All three wings of the house have tall windows facing inward onto the courtyard, thereby providing uninterrupted natural light and a landscape view. The original bedroom/bathroom wing was arranged in a long gallery-like corridor with built-in shelving along the inner wall, between the doors to each bedroom. Windows ran along the opposite side.

RIGHT: Unexpected red-brick wall surfaces faced with wooden trim give the Usonian bathroom a natural warmth that is complemented by the soft quality of the in-built lighting.

In the spacious living area, the inner side of the front wall was also used for built-in shelving and storage integral to the building's fabric. Such features in a Usonian home eliminated the necessity for free-standing furnishings of the client's own taste, and expressed Wright's philosophy that organic architecture alone was the guiding force in all good contemporary design, including that of fixtures and fittings. Wright designed the built-in cypress furniture, although the plywood dining chairs are of Charles Eames' design. The living room extends along a lengthy axis with floor-to-ceiling windows instead of one lateral wall. The original plan for the house showed a generous study area partially secluded behind a second hearth at one end. At the other, the principal hearth is set asymmetrically to one side, allowing a niche for dining to be placed alongside, between the living and utility areas.

The kitchen, renamed by Wright the "work space" in his drawings, was located behind the central hearth, and had an original fireplace of its own. Both its location nearby other family-dominated rooms and its placement within the very central core of the building suggest how seriously Wright meant to challenge traditional, formal notions of domestic life and the serving of meals. He effectively replaced the customarily separate, formal dining space with a more responsive and modern design alternative. Behind the dining area of the Rosenbaum house, the bedroom wing was accessible through the gallery-like corridor.

Wright characteristically organized the interior spaces as open-plan, encouraging easy and informal circulation, and communication between the different functional areas of the home.

ABOVE RIGHT: Wright met the challenges of the Usonian house by tailoring each design to the individual client's needs, creating interiors which could be as cost-effective and functional as possible.

RIGHT: In the Usonian house, Wright centralized the kitchen and dining areas near the principal hearth, arguing that the arrangement was more suitable to families of middle income. The entrance to the kitchen is visible further on from the dining table.

TALIESIN WEST

Constructed: 1937–59
Address: 12621 North Frank Lloyd Wright Boulevard, Scottsdale, Arizona.
Opening hours: Guided tours are offered daily 9am to 4pm.
Telephone: 480-860-8810

From 1938 Wright passed the winters at Taliesin West, a desert site in the Sonora region beneath the McDowell Mountains. He had purchased the land the previous year, envisaging an experimental laboratory and studio. Here he also built his own residence and founded a self-sufficient training and professional community which now houses the Frank Lloyd Wright Foundation and Archives, and the Taliesin Architects professional design group. Wright instituted both the Frank Lloyd Wright School of Architecture and the Taliesin Fellowship, also at the site, in order to continue to train the next generation of aspiring architects. The complex now houses residential quarters, extensive studio space, theaters, and entertaining facilities. The original buildings were nothing more that tent-canvas stretched on redwood trusses. Eventually these were necessarily replaced by more hard-wearing materials, but interior spaces throughout the complex still retain much of the shape and spatial sense of the original tent camp

RIGHT: The Cabaret Theater looking toward the screen and stage area. The ceiling was made of poured concrete and stone, and supported by inward angled trusses with low reliefs of intersecting diagonals. To the end, Wright followed Louis Sullivan's dictum of "organic ornamentation."

The buildings in the complex are largely constructed of fiberglass, steel, and desert rubblestone. Of particular interest is the way in which Wright defined the interior spaces. They are characterized by acutely angled roofs pierced with massive skylights, surrounding glass curtain walls, and sweeping clerestorys. These features combine to flood the rooms with natural light and provide uninterrupted vistas of the landscape that Wright's fertile imagination found so inspiring. The complex is centered around the ninety-six foot by thirty foot drafting studio where one of the major architectural themes is a pronounced juxtaposition of materials. The massing of exposed rubble is set off against the rhythmic truss-work of huge steel beams and rising glass. Wright's experimentation with the dramatic asymmetrical arrangement of highly exaggerated geometric forms and spaces results in interiors which are formed by a series of diagonals. For Wright, these diagonals echoed the patterns of the desert landscape. They express his late susceptibility towards interiors composed of abstract geometric form.

ABOVE RIGHT: The Garden Room was used both formally and informally for social gatherings, and notably includes Wright's "origami" chairs within its furnishings.

RIGHT: The large drafting studio is one of the most spatially compelling features of the complex. Its feel is at once both ephemeral and permanent. The great prow rising upward stretches interior space toward the outlying desert.

ABOVE: The Garden Room "rubblestone" hearth. Construction entailed random collection, then washing of the stone in an acid bath to illuminate the subtle variations in its natural coloring. The stones were then casually arranged and set in poured concrete. This construction process was itself one of the major themes of the architectural aesthetic at Taliesin West.

LOREN POPE HOUSE
(POPE–LEIGHEY HOUSE)

Constructed: 1940
Address: 9000 Richmond Highway, Woodlawn Plantation, Alexandria, Virginia.
Opening hours: Open daily 10am–5pm.
Telephone: 703-780-4000

A superb example of Wright's Usonian-type residence, the design was commissioned by the *Washington Evening Star* journalist Loren Pope as a family home.

Unassuming in scale, the house has a surprisingly spacious interior, composed of three simple elements: wood, glass, and brick. Ceilings are long, flat planes of varying levels, dressed with wooden paneling and containing the recessed lighting so characteristic of Wright's Usonian interiors. Walls and surfaces are treated uniformly throughout, and match the textures and materials (brick and cypress) employed by Wright on the exterior of the building.

The structural and aesthetic core of the house is the unfaced brick hearth. Its importance in the design is echoed by the equally unfaced brick bearing walls at the sides. Together, these features help to establish the Usonian personality of the house as a straight-forward, cost-effective building solution for middle income families. The in-built benches and shelving systems, modular and moveable furnishings, and the fretwork windows are all organically linked to the structure of the building. They share materials (such as simple

RIGHT: The concrete-pad floor containing the heating system is carefully abutted to the brick flooring and walls of the hearth so that there is an unbroken, integrated surface from one feature to another.

plywood), sculptural design and integration of their surfaces. Each element thus reiterates the architectural composition. The ingenious functionality of the modular features, such as the ply chairs, stools, and side tables, is typical of Wright's vision for efficient Usonian interiors in which the living spaces were especially designed not only for comfort but also cost and flexibility of use. Loren Pope himself helped to assemble the interior. Amongst the better-known of Wright's Usonian houses, the Loren Pope interior is often considered the most functionally streamlined and economic.

In 1963, the building's subsequent owner, Mrs. Robert Leighey, gave the house to the National Trust for Historic Preservation when it was threatened with demolition. It was disassembled and transported from its original location to the nearby Woodlawn Plantation where it has been sympathetically reconstructed and restored.

ABOVE RIGHT: The utmost flexibility in the arrangement is made possible by the comfortable and light-weight modular furniture.

ABOVE FAR RIGHT: Even the more private corners of the open-planned living areas of this Usonian house are well-lit and continue to give a spacious and harmonious sense of unity between the interior and exterior of the building.

RIGHT: Despite the overall uniformity of the interior, it is remarkably open and luminous, in part due to Wright's carefully orchestrated combination of lighting. Here he has used a floor-to-ceiling tower of tracery lights, a tracery clerestory, and a window wall, which gives a typically unbroken view of the landscape beyond.

LEFT: Detail view showing the easy blending of natural textures, materials, and surface patterns of the built-in shelves and the sophisticated ribbons of the fretwork clerestory.

LOWELL E. WALTER HOUSE ("CEDAR ROCK")

Constructed: 1945

Address: Cedar Rock, 2611 Quasqueton Diag Boulevard, Quasqueton, Iowa.

Opening hours: Open 11am–4:30pm Tuesday through Sunday.

Telephone: 319-934-3572

Although commissioned in 1942 and designed in 1945, this I-plan Usonian house wasn't occupied until 1950. Its "glass house" design was published by Wright in the *Ladies' Home Journal* also in 1945.

Essentially a summer residence, the main feature of the interior is the dining area, living room, and integral conservatory combined into a single 900 square-foot rectangular space. Tall, running window-walls enclose three sides of the extensive room, providing dramatic views from this eleven-acre hilltop site over the nearby Wapsipinicon River Valley. The natural light also assists the growth of lush indoor foliage in what has often been referred to as the "garden room." The open informality of this space is pronounced. Its innovative design combines what are effectively features of a traditional conservatory with those of a modern family living space. Rooms such as this demonstrate Wright's imaginative response to the individual site of each building, and prove the pedigree of the Usonian house in the organic architecture of his earlier Prairie period.

RIGHT: Waxed, red tile flooring and the dominance of wood finishes are characteristic of Wright's Usonian homes. The generous brick hearth is visible toward the back of the room.

Looking inward through the the the large windows, the elevation of the living area shows how Wright created the movement of space within his interiors. Movement through the room is guided by "invisible" corridors around the edges of the room where there is also seating beneath the protective brick walls and in the seclusion of the overhanging ceiling. The center space serves as a conservatory that can be viewed from all sides. The interior walls are of walnut board-and-batten, while the heating is located in the floor which is typical of a Usonian residence. The hearth remains at the core of the plan. It is the point of departure for the ancillary wing which projects away from the family area at a sharp angle. Bedrooms, bathrooms and utilities are contained there. The kitchen is set just off the living area, but near the hearth, behind a partial brick partition with valuable shelf and storage space above. Wright's vision of the Usonian home included an open kitchen area located near the hearth at the center of the house. This way Wright centralized the working/living spaces and responded to more contemporary lifestyles of much greater informality.

The house has been the property of the Iowa Department of Natural Resources since 1981.

ABOVE RIGHT: The Usonian kitchen, here lying just between the brick parapet, was not a separated room, but open to the activities and necessities of adjacent living and dining areas.

RIGHT: Bedrooms in a Usonian house were characteristically lit by a clerestory, had integral storage, and were aesthetically unified with the rest of the residence by wooden trim and paneling.

LEFT: Here the Usonian clerestory is sheltered beneath a ceiling pierced with skylights. There is also a shallow parapet where indoor plantings can be bathed in indirect natural light.

KENNETH LAURENT HOUSE

Constructed: 1949
Address: Spring Brook Road, Rockford, Illinois.

Designed in 1948, the Laurent house is one of the prime examples of how Wright's sympathetic response to his clients' individual needs determined the chief characteristics of his domestic architecture. In 1948, Kenneth Laurent personally wrote to Wright asking him to design a house. He explained that he was paraplegic and confined to a wheelchair, and had been attracted to Wright's innovative development of the open-plan interior with its generous, uninterrupted, and easily accessible spaces.

The resulting house is a single-story Usonian type—the first of the solar hemicycle houses constructed by Wright. It was designed around the idea of a "football" plan: that is, the slightly elongated shape of an American football laying on its side with the gentle sloping upper and lower curves forming the principle longitudinal axis. The arc of the upper curve is made by the elongated interior gallery which extends nearly the length of the house. The largest bedroom is tucked just off the gallery at one end, and at the other is the living area with the mass of the hearth. The lower curve of the arc forms an exterior landscaped terrace accessible through the broad, floor-to-ceiling glass doorways. The interior space overall is long and low, but

RIGHT: The long interior arc of the "football" plan comprises the wide gallery looking onto the landscaped terrace. It is characteristic of Wright's Usonian houses that there is a very generous length of corridor.

there is a particular focus upon contrasts where the compressed 'refuge' of the gallery suddenly broadens out into the larger space of the living room. There, the horizontal pattern created by the shelving draws attention to how the space expands to the side. Shelving systems and shelved partitions for Wright not only served a functional purpose, but were visual devices which helped to exaggerate the extension of space outward in opposing directions. Principle "rooms" of the house are placed behind the glass gallery and form a sequence of cubes. Each space flows into the next so that movement through the house is by way of the fewest possible number of interior partitions.

Despite the apparent spaciousness of the interior, the house itself is comparatively small. It is constructed largely of conventional brick, with extensive interior woodwork in cypress. Wright's preference for designing individual interior furnishings and integrating them, along with storage units, into the interior fabric was greatly to the client's advantage as it left inner spaces uncluttered and easy to maintain.

OVERLEAF: The two arched sides of the "football" plan are visible here: one formed by the interior of the gallery, the other by the sweeping arch of the terrace wall. Wright sought to eliminate sharp corners in the plan of the house. His intentions were also expressed in the design of the furniture.

DR. ISADORE J. ZIMMERMAN HOUSE

Constructed: 1950

Address: 223 Heather Street, Manchester, New Hampshire.

Opening hours: Tours Thursday, Friday & Monday at 2pm; Saturday & Sunday at 1pm.

Telephone: 603-626-4158

For the Zimmermans, Wright designed what he himself referred to as "a classic Usonian," although in fact the house is more complex than the earlier Usonians. The building is constructed of cypress, cast sand-hued concrete, and brick. Not unusually at this period in his working life, Wright also designed fixtures, fittings, household implements such as dinnerware, and textiles for the house, as well as its furniture, both built-in and free-standing.

The entry facade boasts a horizontal band of pierced concrete blocks which, in the interior, function as a raised band of ribbon windows above continuous built-in benches. The blocks emphasize the low horizontality of the single-story dwelling, and are a further example of Wright's frequent experimentation with the placement of fenestration. The rear side of the living area faces onto a partially landscaped garden also planned by Wright. Here, the interior window bays are formed by tall brick piers which angle into the space of the room, with low brick planting boxes beneath. In the center of each bay Wright hung a wood-framed window surrounded by smaller vertical and horizontal fixed glass panes set into the brick itself. In this area of the house the structural, sculptural quality of the building is pronounced, allowing an easy flow between the exterior and interior of the room with the glass "partitions" acting, as much as anything, as a symbolic barrier. This feeling of inside-outside is enhanced by the five sets of French doors beneath a running clerestory in the dining space.

Since 1988 the house has belonged to the Currier Gallery of Art which carried out the conservation and restoration of the building.

RIGHT: The pitch and finish of the ceiling is contiguous with the underside of the roof outside. This treatment draws the viewer's attention toward the inner rise of the tent-like ceiling space.

a Walls made up of running windows are a consistent feature at the back of Wright''s houses, affording extensive views of gardens and landscape beyond.

b The curving 'arc' not only creates an unusual and pleasant space, but gives an ease of access from one end of the house to the other.

c On the whole, sharp corners are eliminated, enabling freer and safer movement through the house.

d The rhythm of horizontal bands repeats the pattern made by the shelving. Such bands are an excellent example of how Wright integrated 'ornamentation' into the very fabric of a building.

e The simple geometric form of the table betrays Wright's preference for furniture designed using machine-cut pieces.

f Built-in shelving and storage had been an important feature at Wright's domestic interiors from the earliest years of his architectural career.

ABOVE & LEFT: The interior is composed of broad spaces, and the "doorways" throughout are of greater than normal width. The terrace of the Laurent House shows the exterior of the "arc."

ABOVE: Cherokee red tiling beneath the carpets hides Wright's unique "gravity heat" system which is located in the concrete floor slab. He employed the system in residences built in colder climates. The far bay of the room was reserved for music, accommodating the piano and a music stand that Wright based upon one he had designed earlier for his own house.

LEFT: The small, informal dining area is tucked into a nook between, on the one hand, the "protective" side of the brick fireplace and, on the other hand, the "exposed" area where French doors open directly onto a large terrace outside.

RIGHT: Pierced, sand-colored concrete blocks give a bold pattern to the interior. They also illuminate the interior with natural light and are a further development on the theme of Wright's California "textile-block" construction.

HAROLD C. PRICE
COMPANY TOWER

Constructed: 1953–56
Address: Northeast Sixth Street at Dewey Avenue, Bartlesville, Oklahoma.
Opening hours: Guided 45 minute tours; large groups by appointment with
Landmark Preservation Council, Box 941, Bartlesville, Oaklahoma.
Telephone: 918-661-7471

This building was commissioned by Harold C. Price in 1952 as the company headquarters for his oil pipeline construction business, and Wright also designed residences in Bartlesville, in 1953, and in Paradise Valley, Arizona, in 1954, for the Price family. The tower is one of Wright's most significant post-war designs for an office development, and has been owned by Phillips Petroleum since 1981.

Wright envisaged the tower to serve multiple uses, designing its interior to accommodate not only the company headquarters, but also an arrangement of offices and apartments. A redevelopment of an unexecuted design of 1929, the Price building has nineteen floors and is 186 feet tall. Wright designed the tower using the structural and visual metaphor of a tree. Each floor is cantilevered outward on a concrete slab from a steel-reinforced concrete core. As the building rises, the floor area noticeably increases as the tree's "canopy" grows upward and outward. The interior modules above are thus larger than those below. The tower's interior is vertically separated into its different functions. The two-story base serves as an entryway and reception area for the activities above.

The interior elevations of some of the upper floors are opened up vertically to create eight, two-storey offices within the tower. Other floors above are generally divided into four separate diamond-shaped modules comprising offices as well as apartments. One quadrant per floor is given over to an apartment, while the others are devoted to office space betraying the primary function of the building.

RIGHT: The strong angular geometry of Wright's favoured diamond motif unites the surface ornamentation throughout, even including the copper-stamped cladding and chimney, and the inset ceiling lights.

Many interior rooms project into a glass bay at the corners of the building. Thus these comparatively smaller rooms are opened out into the skyline by angled windows. A distinction between residential and office spaces is also made clear on the exterior of the building. Professional spaces are distinguished by horizontal copper-faced louvers (a series of narrow openings), while residential use is signaled by vertical louvering.

The top-most, nineteenth storey holds Harold C. Price's own office, which also has a private rooftop garden, providing the interior with fresh air and a dramatic view over the city and its surrounding landscape. The garden is enclosed by a series of vertical copper-faced louvers, which act like an ornamental protective screen. The space thus becomes more of a room than an exposed rooftop terrace, and is characteristic of Wright's blending of interior and exterior spaces into room-like configurations.

Again, Wright took responsibility for the overall decorative design of the interior and its unique, custom-made furnishings. The feel throughout is for the angular and sharp, with planes and surfaces intersecting unexpectedly. The diamond-shaped module which governs the shape of all the rooms also governs the angular shape of all fittings and fixtures, built-in furnishings and wall treatments.

ABOVE RIGHT: Interior view showing how the simplified geometric forms of the furniture are rhythmically set into the very fabric of the wall.

RIGHT: View showing how interior space of a room juts into the angled side of the window wall.

LEFT: Custom-designed hanging lamps and furnishings, including Wright's so-called "dentist's chair," repeat the diamond motif and complement the angular patterns of the Wright-designed murals.

DONALD & VIRGINIA LOVNESS HOUSE

Constructed: 1955

Address: 10121 83rd North, Stillwater, Minnesota.

One of approximately ten structures designed and built by Wright in Minnesota, this single-story cottage was one of the last of the Usonians. It is roughly square in plan, built of wood and stone, with the hearth situated characteristically at the center. A romantic "single-room" house in concept, the bedrooms are discreetly tucked away in small wings in the back. Closely adhering to Wright's plans, the Lovnesses constructed the house and furnishings themselves, demonstrating how much the architect joined with his clients in launching an assault on the increasing costs of building a well-designed, individualized home.

The dimensions of the house are unconventional. The walls were erected of indigenous buff stone slabs, which lend a protective, subterranean quality to the interior. Remaining walls were largely made of running glass panels with a clerestory beneath the dramatic overhanging eaves. The roof and interior ceiling are constructed as a single extending piece with the inner horizontal joists patterned in brick-like fashion. The interior elevation is relatively low, increasing the impression of security despite the open, almost unobstructed view of the wooded landscape outside. In essence, the house maintains the now familiar pattern of the Usonian

RIGHT: The dining area rests in a glass-enclosed alcove beneath the eaves of the roof. The built-in desk-cum-breakfast table is a greatly simplified variation of the integral sideboards of the much earlier Prairie houses. The surface is illuminated by the wall-lamp based upon a previous Midway Gardens theme.

home with the abundant mass of its centralized hearth, running bands of windows, and prominent terrace directly outside. Characteristically of Wright, the feeling of privacy inside is contrasted to an immediate view of both nearby foliage and distant space. The interior, however, also recalls the exoticism of surface texture and pattern in Wright's Midway Gardens design and the earliest "textile-block" houses in California. This impression is enhanced by the sculptural furnishings of the residents themselves. The house is simply, but richly furnished with benches, chairs, tables, and lamps of Wright's design, all lending themselves to the comparatively straight-forward assembly from precut pieces. The high-backed dining chairs closely resemble those also found in the John Raywad House in New Canaan, Connecticut, of the mid-1950s. They are highly architectural in form and together create a running pattern of latticed "pillars" surrounding the horizontal dining table.

ABOVE RIGHT: The standing lamps at either end of the table are further developments of Wright's dining-table lamps for the Prairie Houses. Their Japanese-inspired design reflects the breadth of influences which continued to surface during the course of his career.

RIGHT: Wright's decorative detailing was consistently in complete harmony with the house and furnishings. The lamp design is derived from the standing garden terrace light originally conceived for Wright's Midway Gardens.

LEFT: The opposite end of the glassed living area demonstrates the dramatic landscape views which were such an important part of Wright's conception of interior space.

DR. GEORGE ABLIN HOUSE

Constructed: 1958

Address: 4260 Country Club Drive, Bakersfield, California.

One of the last commissions undertaken by Wright in California, the Ablin House is Usonian in feel, but marks Wright's continuing experimentation with concrete block construction. In plan, it is a further refinement of his use of the triangular module which governed, among others, the Price Company Tower.

The south-facing wall of the living area is primarily composed of glass. It encloses a series of large bays outlined with Wright's characteristic wooden trim. In the dining area, the vertical walls of the masonry core act as sculptural columns which rise up to meet the sloping ceiling and are offset by the horizontality of the built-in benches, cupboards, and the overhang of the lowered ceiling panel. The angle of the roof extends through the whole of the space, producing a sequence of interior bays, which differ in both height and depth, and continue beyond the large glass pane of the terrace wall. To further enhance its soaring effect, lights are inset into the lower ceilings, accentuating the room's space at a median height and thus setting off the floating quality of the roof above. The living area contains some of Wright's later designs for free-standing furniture; the faceted, abstract construction betraying the maturity of the designer's vision.

RIGHT: The kitchen is of simplified design and efficient in use. Its view directly onto the pool and terrace suggest Wright considered these two areas in direct relationship to one another, associating food preparation with the enjoyment of sport, outside leisure, and entertaining.

The dining and living areas, and the kitchen form the core of the house. Two wings extend laterally, containing the bedrooms and study areas. The kitchen space is centralized and set into a projecting bay constructed of salmon-colored, pierced concrete blocks inset with glass. These create an unusual interplay of light and texture, and face onto the poolside terrace where the moving water of the pool would enhance the effect with ever-changing reflections. The unusual color tones are repeated throughout the house, including in the kitchen tiling, and blend with the wooden surfaces. The house ably demonstrates what Wright could achieve with common, sensibly priced materials. The pierced concrete blocks are treated in masterful fashion, producing a strong sculptural feel to the house while also serving important functional purposes.

ABOVE: The living room includes examples of Wright's angled modular furniture constructed of comparatively inexpensive materials.

RIGHT: The dining area boasts a lowered ceiling panel for greater intimacy. There is also a variation of the theme of the high-backed chair which characterized Wright's dining room furnishings throughout his career.

GAZETTEER

CHARNLEY–PERSKY HOUSE (JAMES A. CHARNLEY HOUSE)

Constructed: 1891
Address: 1365 North Astor Street, Chicago, Illinois.
Opening hours: National Historic Landmark. Public tours April–Nov,
Wednesday 12 pm, & Saturday 12 & 1 pm;
groups over 10 require reservations.
Telephone: 312-915-0105

Through the benefaction of Seymour H. Persky the house became the headquarters of the Society of Architectural Historians in 1995. The interior bears the influence of Louis Sullivan in the second floor, open loggia which rises toward a central skylight in the midsection of the house. The rhythm of basic lines and shapes, however, already expresses the young Wright's vision of light interiors made up of intersecting planes and spaces.

GEORGE BLOSSOM HOUSE

Constructed: 1892
Address: 4858 Kenwood Avenue, Chicago, Illinois.

Among the so-called "bootleg" houses, the interior demonstrates Wright's own emerging style of "organic" architecture. The vertical screen of spindles above the built-in settle acts as a "transparent" partition between the sitting room and the stairwell behind. It is one of Wright's earliest uses of this ornamental 'screen' motif which is incorporated into the very fabric of the house.

W. IRVING CLARKE HOUSE

Constructed: 1893
Address: LaGrange, Illinois.

Another "bootleg" house, the delicate foliage motifs and beading incorporated into the woodwork of the newel post again demonstrate the influence of Louis Sullivan's theories of "organic" ornamentation on Wright. The simple, but fluid decorative carving throughout also bears the imprint of Sullivan's ideas.

E. ARTHUR DAVENPORT HOUSE

Constructed: 1901
Address: 559 Ashland Avenue, River Forest, Illinois.

Executed during a brief business partnership with Webster Tomlinson, the unassuming design is entirely Wright's own. The living room closely resembles that illustrated in his second design published in *The Ladies' Home Journal* of 1901, down to the spherical shape and forceful geometry of the signature andirons.

RIGHT: E. Arthur Davenport House study.

FRANCIS W. LITTLE "1" HOUSE (LITTLE–CLARK HOUSE)

Constructed: 1902
Address: 1505 West Moss,
Peoria, Illinois.

The first of two homes the architect
designed for Little, this comfortable,
brick Prairie-style house
incorporated many of Wright's
characteristic interior features,
including an emphasis on the
harmony of natural materials, built-
in serving and storage areas, and
the overall scheme of earthen color
tones visible in the art glass. Some
of the original furnishings Wright
designed for the house can now be
seen in Allentown Art Museum,
Pennsylvania, and in the
Metropolitan Museum, New York.

RIGHT: Francis W. Little "1" House dining room.

GEORGE & DELTA BARTON HOUSE

Constructed: 1903
Address: 118 Summit Avenue, Buffalo, New York.
Opening hours: For guided tours by reservation only see the entry below
for the Darwin Martin House.
Telephone: 716-856-3858

The first of five structures in the Martin Complex to be built on this site, the house was
commissioned by Darwin D. Martin as a home for his sister and brother-in-law. The cross-axial

plan includes the dining, living, and reception rooms on the ground floor. Nominal divisions between these areas result in an intimate, yet largely unbroken Prairie House interior with a typically substantial brick hearth.

DARWIN D. & ISABELLE R. MARTIN HOUSE

Constructed: 1904
Address: 125 Jewett Parkway, Buffalo, New York.
Opening hours: Guided tours of the Martin House Complex: Wednesday at 3pm, Saturday at 10am and 1pm, and Sunday at 1pm. By reservation only through the Martin House Restoration Corporation, Market Arcade, 617 Main Street, Buffalo, New York.
The house is jointly administered by: the New York State Office of Parks, Recreation and Historic Preservation, the State University of New York, and the Martin House Restoration Corporation.
Telephone: 716-856-3858

Commissioned by Martin, who also commissioned the Larkin Company Administration building of 1903, the home is considered one of the finest examples of the Prairie House. Details throughout the interior show how carefully Wright employed abstract, geometric patterning in his decorative schemes to signify natural forms, and how distinctive his own abstract language of ornament was becoming.

HIRAM BALDWIN HOUSE

Constructed: 1905
Address: 205 Essex Road, Kenilworth, Illinois.

A further instance of the Prairie House style, the entrance hallway exemplifies the simplified, geometric clarity of Wright's interiors. Each vertical and horizontal feature has been subtly calculated to create the overall effect of light, welcoming, and semi-transparent interior spaces. The floor-to-ceiling columns of glass were to become an important feature of Wright's interiors.

CHARLES A. BROWN HOUSE

Constructed: 1905
Address: 2420 Harrison Street, Evanston, Illinois.

Perhaps something of a transitional example, the rectangular plan of the building nonetheless shows typical interior characteristics, such as Wright's preference for waxed rather than varnished surfaces, and his desire to rationalize interior spaces into compositions governed by verticals and horizontals.

UNITY TEMPLE

Constructed: 1905
Address: 875 Lake Street at Kenilworth Avenue, Oak Park, Illinois.
Opening hours: Self guided visits possible from 1–4pm daily; guided tours on
Saturday and Sunday at 1, 2, and 3 pm.
Telephone: 708-383-8873

BELOW: Unity Temple.

Designated a National Historic Landmark in 1971, the building was pioneering in American religious architecture for its bold handling of interior space.
The two-story central auditorium is spanned by concrete beams, and composed of a sequence of smaller square and rectangular spaces which flow together. At its highest point the ceiling is almost entirely composed of the coffered skylight, its effect enhanced by the rows of second-story windows. The auditorium is richly ornamented with geometric banding, and tiered seating along both sides helps to lessen the distance between the congregation and the pulpit.

W. H. PETTIT MEMORIAL CHAPEL

Constructed: 1906
Address: Belvidere Cemetery, North Main at Harrison, Belvidere, Illinois.
Opening hours: Viewing of the interior welcome, but by prior reservation.
Telephone: 815-547-7642

This modest and restrained interior, calming in its simplicity, is often overlooked within Wright's works. The cruciform layout is both typical of his Prairie style of the period and suitably symbolic for a chapel of remembrance. A central brick hearth punctuates the strong horizontality of the interior elevation, while high ribbon windows and a judicious application of wooden banding subtly accentuate this intimate space.

DR. GEORGE C. STOCKMAN HOUSE

Constructed: 1908
Address: 530 First Street North East, Mason City, Iowa.
Opening hours: Open to the public much of the year from late May through to the end of October. Guided tours are available on Thursday, Friday, and Saturday between 10am and 5pm, and on Sunday from 1–5pm.
Telephone: 641-42-3666

BELOW: Dr. George C. Stockman House bedroom.

Typical of Wright's smaller and more unassuming Prairie-style homes, the roughly square plan of this house includes four bedrooms on the second floor. Amongst the earliest houses to evolve from his ideas published as "A Fireproof House for $5,000" in the Ladies' Home Journal of 1907, the house was also one of the first in which Wright wrapped the first floor living and dining rooms around a substantial central fireplace into a continuously flowing interior space. The building was moved to its present location in 1989 and restored.

WILLIAM B. GREEN HOUSE

Constructed: 1912
Address: 1300 Garfield Avenue, Aurora, Illinois.

Wright's concept of the common sense domestic building for the American Midwest was based on a belief that the home should be designed to both protect and provide for the specific needs of the inhabitants. This dictated that interiors should be a collection of unified, interpenetrating spaces freed from unnecessary walls which would separate and enclose.

ARTHUR L. RICHARDS HOUSE (BUNGALOW)

Constructed: 1916
Address: 1835 South Layton Street, Milwaukee, Wisconsin.

A number of small-scale buildings were designed by Wright for Richards, including another house and a group of duplex apartments, both in Milwaukee. This house is an example of "design for production"—the buildings' components were designed to be factory pre-cut and assembled on site. The comparatively small dimensions of such buildings, as well as their interior features, made this experiment a viable solution to increasing demands for urban housing.

RIGHT: Arthur L. Richards House seating nook.

HENRY J. & ELSIE ALLEN HOUSE
(ALLEN–LAMBE HOUSE MUSEUM AND STUDY CENTER)

Constructed: 1917
Address: 255 North Roosevelt Avenue, Wichita, Kansas.

Opening hours: Guided tours by advance appointment only.
Telephone: 316-687-1027

Executed while Wright was engaged on the Imperial Hotel, Tokyo, this house was commissioned by Elsie and Henry J. Allen, a journalist, former Kansas State Governor, and US Senator. The house is a late and unusual L-shaped Prairie House. It includes a substantial living room of nearly 1,000 square feet which opens freely onto the terrace, creating strong spatial continuity between the interior and exterior of the building. Interiors throughout are especially elegant in their combinations of cypress, gum, and walnut wood finishes, exposed brickwork with unique gold-leaf pointing, art glass, and furniture designed in collaboration with George Niedecken.

SAMUEL & HARRIET FREEMAN HOUSE

Constructed: 1923
Address: 1962 Glencoe Way, Los Angeles, California.
Opening hours: Owned by the University of Southern California since 1986, the house is now closed indefinitely due to earthquake damage and restoration.
Telephone: 323-851-0671

BELOW: Samuel & Harriet Freeman House sitting room.

One of the four concrete textile-block houses Wright designed in southern California. The interior opens around the focal point of the hearth, but the spaces change dramatically in both height and direction as they move outward in a thoroughly abstract composition. A series of inner vistas give the interior a feeling of greater space than it actually contains. The textured patterns of the textile blocks create a unity of surface ornamentation between the interior and exterior walls, while the impression of spaciousness is enhanced by the changing daylight filtering through the pierced blocks.

HERBERT JACOBS "1" HOUSE

Constructed: 1936
Address: 441 Toepfer Street, Madison, Wisconsin.

The first Usonian house, this welcoming residence has a much abridged Prairie-type interior. The emphasis on wood, brick, and glass effectively links the interior with the exterior of the building and its natural surroundings. Interior surfaces celebrate contrasts between natural textures and colors, and are arranged into overall patterns of horizontal bands. The flat ceiling, built-in furniture, and bookcases are characteristic, lending themselves to an efficient use of limited space.

SIDNEY BAZETT HOUSE (BAZETT–FRANK HOUSE)

Constructed: 1938–40
Address: 101 Reservoir Road, Hillsborough, California.

One of Wright's more modest California residences and his second in San Francisco, the house has a number of Usonian features. The long living and dining room areas share their space in one wing of the house, while the kitchen is at the center of the design and seperated from adjacent areas by simple shelving. The kitchen is efficiently planned with built-in storage, while its clerestory provides ample light and ventilation.

ANNIE PFEIFFER CHAPEL, FLORIDA SOUTHERN UNIVERSITY

Constructed: 1938–54
Address: 111 Lake Hollingsworth Drive, Lakeland, Florida.
Opening hours: Visitors are requested to go to the campus Administration Building before embarking on self-guided tours. Guided tours also available.
Telephone: 863-680-4116

LEFT: Annie Pfeiffer Chapel, Florida Southern University, auditorium.

Ten buildings on the campus were constructed to Wright's designs over twenty years. The complex is dominated by the hexagonally-planned Annie Pfeiffer Chapel constructed in cast concrete and part textile block. The vertical layering of the Chapel's interior spaces is enriched by the contrasting surface textures and pierced block screens. The whole is illuminated from above by angled skylights. As in the earlier Unity Temple, horizontal tiers of seating result a remarkable intimacy between the congregation and the speakers' platform.

GEORGE D. STURGES HOUSE ("SKYEWAY")

Constructed: 1939
Address: 449 Skyeway Drive, Brentwood Heights, Los Angeles, California.

The house is a further example of how the living area represents the most important space for family life within Wright's Usonian residences. Alternating ceiling heights allow for both direct and indirect lighting. The warm effects of the wooden paneling help to create sheltered seating recesses within the open-plan. The house contains examples of Wright's "oragami" chairs.

UNITARIAN MEETING HOUSE

Constructed: 1947
Address: 900 University Bay Drive, Shorewood Hills, Madison, Wisconsin.
Opening hours: Guided tours are available following services or by appointment.
Telephone: 608-233-9774

The rich interior is dominated by the strong textural relief of Wisconsin native limestone and the sloped underside of the prow-shaped roof. Above the pulpit there is the choir balcony. Further above rise the horizontal bands of windows which jut deeply into the pointed gable. The building was considered revolutionary for its time. It is a statement of contrasts between surface textures, dark and light, and a variety of geometric forms, most importantly the triangle upon which the plan itself is based. The strongly rational, yet sheltering atmosphere of the main auditorium creates a particularly suitable sanctuary for the Unitarian faith in which Wright himself was raised.

MAYNARD P. BUEHLER HOUSE

Constructed: 1948
Address: 6 Great Oak Circle,
Orinda, California.

Of wood and concrete block
construction, one of the most
captivating features of this L-plan house
is the butterfly roof which reaches
downward as it spans the living room.
The underside of the roof is rendered
with panels, which continue into the
ceiling of the interior, giving the living
space more the feeling of an outside
terrace. Built-in benches occupy two
sides of the room and merge into the
depth of the room's corner, making that
a fully usable space and emphasizing
the angularity of the floor plan.

ABOVE: Maynard P. Buehler House living room.

CURTIS MEYER HOUSE

Constructed: 1948
Address: 11108 Hawthorne Drive, Galesberg, Michigan.

One of Wright's "Solar Hemicycle" houses designed for more northern climates, like the Eric
Brown House it is constructed of exposed concrete block with one long wall embedded into the
rise of the earth for insulation. The opposite wall is composed of glass doors and windows
facing west. These capture the maximum amount of warmth from the sun and flood the interior
with light. Wright's construction techniques allowed large interior spaces on the ground floor to
be cleared of any structural supports necessary for the roof or upper floors.

ALBERT ADELMAN HOUSE

Constructed: 1948
Address: 7111 North Barnett, Fox Point, Wisconsin.

Wright built two homes for the Adelman family; this one, and another in Phoenix, Arizona. The house is a fine example of how functional furnishings were incorporated as integral features of the home. One of Wright's favorite motifs, the wooden screen, here takes the form of a built-in shelving system which also serves as a transparent partition between key "rooms" of the living area. The simple components could be easily and inexpensively manufactured, representing Wright's preference for design for machine production.

ABOVE: Albert Adelman House living room with open ceiling of wooden beams.

ERIC V. BROWN HOUSE

Constructed: 1949
Address: 2806 Taliesin Drive, Parkwyn Village, Kalamazoo, Michigan.

Constructed of mahogany and textile-block, the interior reveals the structural materials of the house. The dining area projects into one of the lateral bays, while the kitchen is conveniently sited behind the body of the fireplace. The house exemplifies Wright's opening up of domestic interior space, which he pioneered in the Prairie Houses. The simplified, geometric forms of the furniture designed by Wright are thoroughly sympathetic with the architecture, and even mimic the pitch of the sloping ceiling in the living area.

DONALD SCHBERG HOUSE

Constructed: 1950; additions 1960s
Address: 1155 Wrightwind Drive, Okemos, Michigan.

A large house of simple plan in which any sense of confined space is eliminated. Even at this late date in Wright's career, the hearth continues to provide the focal point, yet each unique detail of the house was the result of his ever fertile imagination. Sloping beams and in-built wooden features continued to be some of the most durable motifs of Wright's vision of interior domestic space.

FIRST CHRISTIAN CHURCH

Constructed: 1950
Address: 6750 North Seventh Avenue, Phoenix, Arizona.
Opening hours: Self-guided tours during business hours 8:30am–4:30pm Monday through Friday.
Telephone: 602-246-9206

Originally commissioned in 1949 as a chapel for the university at the Southwest Christian Seminary, the interior was planned on the form of a triangle, symbolic of Christian unity. Not constructed at that time, the project was rekindled in 1970. The inner sanctuary takes the shape of a diamond surmounted by a pyramidal roof with its spire inset with colored glass. This allows light to permeate the interior space constructed of concrete and indigenous stone. The distinctly earthy texture and coloring of these materials contrast sharply with the translucent light flooding in from above. The resulting symbolic quality of the interior is impressive as real space seems to dissolve as it rises towards the apex of the ceiling.

ABOVE: First Christian Church interior ceiling expanse above seating.

FRANK LLOYD WRIGHT'S FIELD OFFICE, SAN FRANCISCO

Constructed: 1951
Address: In 1992 the office became part of the Heinz Architectural Center, Carnegie Museum of Art, 4400 Forbes Avenue, Pittsburgh, Pennsylvania.
Opening hours: Can be visited during normal Museum hours 9am–4:30 Monday to Friday.
Telephone: 412-622-3289

The design was conceived in collaboration with the former student at Taliesin and practicing architect, Aaron Green, who

ABOVE: Frank Lloyd Wright's Field Office, San Francisco.

shared the office and acted as Wright's field supervisor for works carried out in California. Originally a 900 square foot space, the interior was "partitioned" by plywood louvers and running glass panes which served to define separate work spaces. The drafting room shows Usonian characteristics, including the red vinyl floor tiling and the extensive redwood ply woodwork. Redwood is a native California resource and, typical of Wright's common sense, functional aesthetic, was not only an indigenous material, but at that time was readily available and not expensive.

KAREN JOHNSON HOUSE (JOHNSON–KELAND HOUSE)

Constructed: 1954
Address: 1425 Valley View Drive, Racine, Wisconsin.

Built for the daughter of the owner of Johnson Wax, H.F. Johnson. Wright also designed the Johnson Administration Building and "Wingspread" for this family. The axial hallway was a fundamental, albeit often overlooked, feature of Wright's domestic design. This example is typical in the reflective Cherokee Red tile flooring, doorways to bedrooms, and other more private areas opening off one side only, rows of windows looking onto the landscape or garden along the opposite side and, not unusually, ample built-in storage.

BETH SHOLOM SYNAGOGUE

Constructed: 1954
Address: 8231 Old York Road, Elkins Park, Pennsylvania.
Opening hours: Guided tours by appointment.
Telephone: 215-887-1342

The great sanctuary of the synagogue is celebrated for the symbolic intricacy of its design. Interior, exterior, and plan resulted from a collaboration between Wright and the congregation's Rabbi, Mortimer J. Cohen. The roof's interior is faced with corrugated plastic; the exterior with reinforced glass. Daylight—signifying the gift of divine law—emanates through the faceted surfaces of the pyramid atop the hexagonal roof, itself signifying Mount Sinai. Symbolic devices surround the pulpit, including the "stone tablets" of the concrete monolith, the wooden ark enclosing scrolls of the Torah, and the sculpture surmounting the ark.

HOFFMAN AUTO SHOWROOM (MERCEDES–BENZ MANHATTAN)

Constructed: 1954
Address: 430 Park Avenue at 56th Street, New York, New York.
Opening hours: There are no organized tours. Visitors are welcome, but it is asked that business is respectfully considered.
Telephone: 212-629-1666

Perhaps a surprisingly impersonal interior from the originator of the Prairie and Usonian houses, this showroom and office nevertheless indicate how responsive Wright could be to individual client's needs. The original commission was from Maximilian Hoffman who imported luxury automobiles from Europe to the American market during the early post-war period. The commission allowed Wright to plan an efficient as well as sophisticated open office space which still provided each customer with a sense of privacy. The showroom has been the home of Mercedes–Benz Manhattan from 1957.

DOROTHY H. TURKEL HOUSE

Constructed: 1955
Address: 2760 West Seven Mile Road, Detroit, Michigan.

Unusually for Wright, windows are entirely absent in this extraordinary home. The house was constructed of pierced blocks not unlike those used earlier by Wright in his textile-block houses in California. Natural light is thus admitted through the very structure of the house, which is the only two-story Usonian "automatic" to have been built. Another distinct feature of the interior is the living room which has a two-story elevation.

KALITA HUMPHRIES THEATER

Constructed: 1955
Address: Dallas Theater Center, 3636 Turtle Creek Boulevard, Dallas, Texas.
Opening hours: Tours during working hours 9am to 5pm by appointment only.
Telephone: 214-526-8210

The only theater to have been commissioned and completed based upon Wright's designs for this type of building, it is an adaptation of his earlier ideas. In addition to containing an open-planed auditorium with a circular stage and balconies, the building comprises an unusual cylindrical drum which itself contains the stage with a rotating platform at its center.

KARL KUNDERT MEDICAL CLINIC

Constructed: 1955
Address: 1106 Pacific Street, San Luis Obispo.

An often overlooked example of Wright's designs for small professional offices, this should be considered in the same category as

RIGHT: Karl Kundert Medical Clinic.

the Meyers Medical Clinic of the same year in Dayton, Ohio, and the Lockridge Medical Clinic of 1958 in Whitefish, Montana. Here, the interior is influenced by the Usonian House type, and has an equally warm domestic feel. Walls are faced with timber paneling, lighting fixtures are recessed, and the overall scheme reduced to simplified, easy to manufacture, geometric shapes. The high clerestory with fretwork windows and gabeled ceiling keep the small reception area from seeming too enclosed. The ply reception desk is clearly of Wright's design.

CARL POST HOUSE (BORAH–POST HOUSE)

Constructed: 1956
Address: 265 Donlea Road, Barrington Hills, Illinois.

During the course of his career, Wright designed suburban houses of varying cost, scale, and complexity. This prefabricated L-plan house for the Marshall Erdman Company was yet another innovation. The entryway and the living room with hearth are located at the junction of the two wings of the "L," at the symbolic and actual center of the home, while additional rooms are distributed along the wings. Although "ready-made," the house remains a complete statement of Wright's design principles, including his dictum that all architectural decoration was to be an integral part of the surface of the house.

ROBERT G. WALTON HOUSE

Constructed: 1957
Address: 417 Hogue Road, Modesto, California.

The dining area of this T-plan Usonian house clearly reveals the undisguised surfaces of the concrete blocks which Wright used for the construction. It also contains one variation of the signature high-backed dining chairs and table for which Wright's interiors are so well known. The sculptural forms and arrangement of these pieces derive from Wright's early use of similar examples in the Prairie Houses and represent his belief that dining signified the core values of family life.

CARL SCHULTZ HOUSE

Constructed: 1957
Address: 2704 Highland Court, Saint Joseph, Michigan.

Constructed from reclaimed bricks at the behest of the owner, the house was incomplete at the time of Wright's death and was finished by his associates at Taliesin. Utility areas in Wright's houses are fundamentally practical and simplified in their plan in order to easily serve a variety of personal needs. Here, the tall windows provide plenty of natural light and ventilation, and the small in-built shelving system has been designed in juxtaposition to the ample cupboard storage.

ABOVE: Carl Schultz House kitchen.

MARIN COUNTY CIVIC CENTER

Constructed: 1957
Address: North San Pedro Road at U.S. Interstate 101, San Rafael, California.
Opening hours: One-hour guided tours; group tours by appointment.
Telephone: 415-456-3276

The only civic government building to be executed by Wright, construction was not complete at the time of his death. It was later completed to plan by his architectural associates, and is a further development of the civic scheme he originally envisaged during the 1930s for the utopian Broadacre City project. Wright's two main features for this, at that time, pastoral site were to be a California State Government Hall of Justice and Administration Building, both long, axial structures with central atriums. The atriums were to be exposed to the sky. Later reconsiderations, however, led to the spanning of these open spaces by

BELOW: Marin County Civic Center atrium.

barrel-vaulted skylights. There remains, however, more than enough natural illumination for the monolithic, concrete planters and for the long, arcaded galleries off which there are offices.

PILGRIM CONGREGATIONAL CHURCH

Constructed: 1958
Address: 2850 Foothill Boulevard, Redding, California.
Opening hours: Open for public viewing Monday through Friday 9am–4pm.
Telephone: 530-243-3121

A further example of Wright's use of the angular-shaped module during the later phases of his career. The structure is of a triangular plan with a low metal roof suspended on concrete supports hovering above the principal sanctuary. Walls were fabricated from rubblestone originating in the desert, a material also used by Wright in California at the low-lying Robert Berger House of 1950 in San Anselmo. The use of rubblestone both inside and out helps identity the building as a late expression of Wright's continuing arts and crafts aesthetic which valued the use of undisguised, regional materials. Inside, the triangular motif is repeated in decorative detailing of the wooden ceiling, colored glass, and floor tiling.

GRADY GAMMAGE MEMORIAL AUDITORIUM

Constructed: 1959
Address: Arizona State University, Apache Boulevard at Mill Avenue, Tempe, Arizona.
Opening hours: Guided tours Monday through Friday at 1, 2, and 3pm, but telephone
ahead as tours are not available during rehearsals or performances.
Telephone: 480-965-4050

The last public space to be constructed to Wright's design, this center for the performing arts comprises a proscenium theater, concert hall, offices, and teaching facilities. The auditorium building was planned in the shape of a large, circular drum. Its interior is divided into two smaller circular areas. The first and largest holds the audience hall, promenade corridors, and glass-walled lobbies, while the smaller circle comprises ancillary and administrative rooms and the stage. The circular theme also governs many of the building's details. Unfinished at the time of Wright's death, completion of the interior was supervised from Taliesin.

INDEX